SURVIVE IN THE DESERT WITH THE FRENCH FOREIGN LEGION

ELITE FORCES SURVIVAL GUIDE SERIES

Elite Survival
Survive in the Desert with the French Foreign Legion
Survive in the Arctic with the Royal Marine Commandos
Survive in the Mountains with the U.S. Rangers and Army
    Mountain Division
Survive in the Jungle with the Special Forces "Green Berets"
Survive in the Wilderness with the Canadian and Australian
    Special Forces
Survive at Sea with the U.S. Navy SEALs
Training to Fight with the Parachute Regiment
The World's Best Soldiers

Elite Operations and Training
Escape and Evasion
Surviving Captivity with the U.S. Air Force
Hostage Rescue with the SAS
How to Pass Elite Forces Selection
Learning Mental Endurance with the U.S. Marines

Special Forces Survival Guidebooks
Survival Equipment
Navigation and Signaling
Surviving Natural Disasters
Using Ropes and Knots
Survival First Aid
Trapping, Fishing, and Plant Food
Urban Survival Techniques

SURVIVE IN THE DESERT WITH THE FRENCH FOREIGN LEGION

CHRIS McNAB

**Introduction by Colonel John T. Carney. Jr., USAF–Ret.
President, Special Operations Warrior Foundation**

MASON CREST PUBLISHERS

This edition first published in 2003
by Mason Crest Publishers Inc.
370 Reed Road, Broomall, PA, 19008

Library of Congress Cataloging-in-Publication Data available

ISBN 1-59084-001-1

Editorial and design by
Amber Books Ltd.
Bradley's Close
74–77 White Lion Street
London N1 9PF

Project Editor Chris Stone
Designer Simon Thompson
Picture Research Lisa Wren

Printed and bound in Malaysia

10 9 8 7 6 5 4 3 2 1

ACKNOWLEDGMENT
For authenticating this book, the Publishers would like to thank the Public Affairs Offices of the U.S. Special Operations Command, MacDill AFB, FL.; Army Special Operations Command, Fort Bragg, N.C.; Navy Special Warfare Command, Coronado, CA.; and the Air Force Special Operations Command, Hurlbert Field, FL.

IMPORTANT NOTICE
The survival techniques and information described in this publication are for use in dire circumstances where the safety of the individual is at risk. Accordingly, the publisher cannot accept any responsibility for any prosecution or proceedings brought or instituted against any person or body as a result of the uses or misuses of the techniques and information within.

DEDICATION
This book is dedicated to those who perished in the terrorist attacks of September 11, 2001, and to the Special Forces soldiers who continually serve to defend freedom.

Picture Credits
Corbis: 20, 22, 28, 29, 36, 40, 42, 46, 48, 49, 58, 61, 66, 87; **Military Picture Library:** 31, 88
TRH: 6, 8, 10, 11, 12, 14, 16, 31, 32/33, 38, 44, 56, 63, 73, 76, 78, 79, 82, 84
Illustrations courtesy of Amber Books and De Agostini UK
Front cover: **TRH** (inset), **Corbis** (main)

CONTENTS

11 JUL 2005

INTRODUCTION

Elite forces are the tip of Freedom's spear. These small, special units are universally the first to engage, whether on reconnaissance missions into denied territory for larger, conventional forces or in direct action, surgical operations, preemptive strikes, retaliatory action, and hostage rescues. They lead the way in today's war on terrorism, the war on drugs, the war on transnational unrest, and in humanitarian operations as well as nation building. When large scale warfare erupts, they offer theater commanders a wide variety of unique, unconventional options.

Most such units are regionally oriented, acclimated to the culture and conversant in the languages of the areas where they operate. Since they deploy to those areas regularly, often for combined training exercises with indigenous forces, these elite units also serve as peacetime "global scouts" and "diplomacy multipliers," a beacon of hope for the democratic aspirations of oppressed peoples all over the globe.

Elite forces are truly "quiet professionals": their actions speak louder than words. They are self-motivated, self-confident, versatile, seasoned, mature individuals who rely on teamwork more than daring-do. Unfortunately, theirs is dangerous work. Since "Desert One"—the 1980 attempt to rescue hostages from the U.S. embassy in Tehran, for instance—American special operations forces have suffered casualties in real world operations at close to fifteen times the rate of U.S. conventional forces. By the very nature of the challenges which face special operations forces, training for these elite units has proven even more hazardous.

Thus it's with special pride that I join you in saluting the brave men and women who volunteer to serve in and support these magnificent units and who face such difficult challenges ahead.

Colonel John T. Carney, Jr., USAF–Ret.
President, Special Operations Warrior Foundation

The hat worn by this legionnaire is called a kepi. Private rank soldiers wear a white kepi while officers are allowed to wear a black version.

THE LEGION FROM THE DESERT

They were originally criminals, beggars, and adventurers. Today the French Foreign Legion is a respected, well-armed, and elite fighting force.

Disciplined, highly trained, and motivated, the Legion is one of the toughest units you could ever meet. They have fought all over the world—from the battlefields of Europe in World War II to the jungles of what is now Vietnam. However, they have a special relationship with the desert. The Legion was born in the deserts of North Africa. For much of their history they were based in a camp at Sidi-bel-Abbès, Algeria, their headquarters for many years. There are no better soldiers from whom to learn the techniques for surviving in the world's desert climates.

The concept of the French Foreign Legion was created after the French revolution of 1830, and the Legion was actually formed by royal command in March 1831. Officially, only foreigners between the ages of 18 and 40 years were allowed to join. In reality, the Legion took almost anyone because France's new king, Louis-Philippe, wanted to use it to remove the country's unemployed soldiers who were thought to be dangerous. Poor citizens and felons left workhouses and prisons to join the Legion's ranks. Dressed in

Captain Danjou is one of the Legion's most legendary figures. He lost a hand fighting in the Crimean War in Europe in the 1850s.

ragged uniforms, both young and old were loaded onto ships for the arduous journey to Algeria, a French colony in North Africa. Once there, they were put to work building and repairing roads. This was the Legion's humble birth.

However, the Legion soon showed that they were good fighters. One incident shows us the resilient spirit of the early Legion. In 1863, the Foreign Legion found itself in Mexico protecting the government of the Emperor Maximilian. On April 29, 63 legionnaires under the command of a Captain Danjou were escorting a shipment of gold bullion—a dangerous job. Without warning, they were attacked by over 2,000 Mexican rebels at the deserted village of Camerone, near Puebla.

Every year on 30 April, the wooden hand of Captain Danjou is paraded by the Legion in memory of the battle of Camerone in Mexico.

Camerone, 1863, where the Legion fought 2000 Mexican soldiers. At one point the legionnaires had nothing to eat or drink for over 24 hours.

The legionnaires were assaulted by a force of cavalry in the early hours of the morning. Using their rifles, bayonets, and swords, they managed to repel it. Yet in the confusion of battle, the mules carrying their water and ammunition had bolted, leaving them with almost no supplies. Danjou ordered a retreat to a deserted farmhouse. Once there, the legionnaires patiently awaited the next attack. Sixteen legionnaires had been killed in the first action, leaving Captain Danjou with only 47 men under his command. However, Danjou had confidence in his men's courage and marksmanship. The Mexicans asked the legionnaires to surrender. This offer was curtly rejected, and Danjou took a promise from each man that he would fight to the death.

The badge of the 13th Foreign Legion Half Brigade which fought in Norway and Egypt during World War II.

The Mexicans renewed their attack and were met by a hail of rifle fire; at around 11 A.M. Danjou himself was killed. At noon the Mexicans were reinforced by another 1,000 infantrymen. By 5 P.M. there were only 11 legionnaires left alive. An hour later there were only six legionnaires left standing, and they had no ammunition for their rifles. Using only their

Because the Legion recruits from all over the world, some World War II legionnaires found themselves fighting their own countrymen.

bayonets, they charged the Mexican positions, to be met by a storm of bullets that killed three of them and stopped the rest. A Mexican colonel stepped forward and demanded their surrender. They replied that they would do so only if they were allowed to keep their weapons and tend to their wounded. The colonel replied, "One can refuse nothing to men like you."

By the end of World War I, the Legion was known throughout the world as a fearsome fighting unit. Each legionnaire was part of the Legion "family," though it was a family with very harsh discipline. Eighty years after its formation, the Legion had grown from a ragtag rabble to a crack fighting force.

World War II was a very difficult time for the Legion. France was split between those who wanted to cooperate with the German occupiers (this was known as the "**Vichy**" regime), and those who wanted to get rid of them. Because of this, some legionnaires were

THE LEGION FAMILY

When a person joins the Legion, he/she becomes a member of an entirely new family. For the first few months of training the legionnaires are allowed little or no contact with their parents or relatives, and they also have to hand in all their personal belongings when they arrive at training camp. They are allowed no visitors. The training that follows is brutal, and the discipline is extremely tough. But if they can survive, then the Legion will look after them for the rest of their lives.

Legionnaires in Africa stop to consult their maps. All military maps are divided up into a grid, and the grid lines are numbered along the top and side of the map. These numbers are called coordinates.

forced into fighting for the Germans, and even fought other legionnaires who sided with the United States and Britain. Eventually, the Vichy government surrendered, and the Legion came together as a family again at Sidi-bel-Abbès. They subsequently battled hard against the Germans in the deserts of Libya and Egypt, and showed that they were fearless men.

After the war, many legionnaires were sent to fight in the jungles of what is now known as Vietnam, but what was then called **Indochina**. Indochina was a French colony that was occupied by the Japanese during the war. Following the end of World War II, and the surrender of the Japanese, many of Indochina's citizens did not want the French back. So they formed an army—known as the **Viet Minh**—and started a war to expel the French from their country.

The legionnaires were sent into the thick of the fighting, and they showed their amazing courage once again. On July 25, 1948, 104 legionnaires were attacked at Phu Tong Hoa in the remote Cao Bang mountains. After bombarding the fort with **mortars** and artillery, thousands of Viet Minh launched human-wave attacks on three sides, flooding into it through a hole smashed in the wall. The gap was held by only one legionnaire, Sergeant Huegen, armed with a **machine gun**. Legionnaires who joined him were killed in the fighting.

By nighttime Huegen was dead, but the courtyard was again cleared with a bayonet charge. As the remaining legionnaires prepared for the next savage onslaught, the clouds parted, illuminating the fort with bright moonlight. Unable to approach the fort unseen, the Vietnamese, many of their soldiers killed, withdrew into the night.

This was a Legion victory, but other actions were disastrous. In November 1953, legionnaire paras were dropped into a valley called Dien Bien Phu to reinforce a French outpost. The French base

Legionnaires on parade. The kepi hat is now worn only on ceremonial occasions. In combat it is replaced by a green commando beret.

appeared to be impregnable. It was protected by a series of heavily defended strongpoints, and was garrisoned by over 16,000 men, over 5,000 of them legionnaires.

On March 13, the Viet Minh attacked. With astonishing strength, they had managed to drag heavy artillery weapons high up into the jungle-covered mountains. From here they could shell the French and remain hidden from French aircraft by the dense foliage. The Viet Minh completely outnumbered the French, and they attacked ferociously. The Legion fought valiantly, killing and wounding hundreds of Viet Minh. Over the next few weeks, Vietnamese losses rose to 20,000 men, compared to French losses of just 7,184 men killed or wounded. Despite this, on May 7, 1954, it was the French who were forced to surrender. Though they had lost the battle, the Legion had proved once again its incredible will to fight. It was one of the saddest, yet proudest, moments in the Legion's history. Following the battle at Dien Bien Phu, the French were forced to leave Indochina.

After Indochina, the Legion went straight from the jungle back to the desert. On the day that Dien Bien Phu fell, Algerian guerrillas called the Algerian National Liberation Army (**ALN**) began a war to throw the French out of Algeria like the Vietnamese had done in Indochina. Many French and Algerian people were massacred, and the Legion was sent in to restore order.

In the harsh desert countryside of Algeria, units of legionnaires hunted down the various ALN units. Their desert survival skills were often required as they spent days under the baking heat of the African sun. Companies of legionnaires were lifted into guerrilla-held areas by Sikorsky S-58 and Boeing-Vertol H-21 ("flying banana") helicopters.

When the enemy was found, the legionnaires would quickly surround them, tossing grenades into the undergrowth. Guerrillas who survived the grenades and ran were shot down by machine guns as they desperately tried to escape from the Legion.

Though the Legion was very successful with this tactic, it was eventually decided that Algeria would be better granted its independence; the rebellion was costing France too much. This brought in a new era for the Legion, and it settled in mainland France. However, the Legion has continued to be involved with events in Africa. In 1969, legionnaires were back in Africa, fighting in Chad, a country that needed French help to fight off two guerrilla armies. The fighting took place in the arid mountains and deserts in the north of the country. Once more the Legion used helicopters to fight with mobility and speed, and battle was fierce. In September 1969, a group of legionnaires was airlifted to Faya-Largeau, where the Chadian Army had been attacked by a large force of rebels. The guerrillas withdrew into remote desert mountains, and the legionnaires went straight after them. Many guerrillas were hunted down by the Legion. Those that were left retreated into caves deep in the mountains. Even there they were not safe, and the legionnaires flushed them out with explosives and bullets.

The Foreign Legion helped defeat the rebel forces, and they later returned to Chad in March 1978 to train and lead the Chadian Army against other rebel forces in the country. Later the Legion saw two other significant operations in Africa. On April 3, 1976, legionnaire paratroops helped rescue French children from a terrorist-held bus on the Djibouti-Somalia border. Two years later,

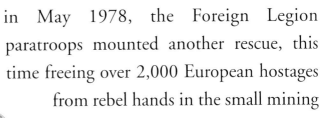

in May 1978, the Foreign Legion paratroops mounted another rescue, this time freeing over 2,000 European hostages from rebel hands in the small mining town of Kolwezi, in Zaire.

History shows that the Legion has never been separated for long from the desert. Legion troops fought alongside the U.S. 82nd Airborne Division during the Gulf War in 1991 in the deserts of Kuwait and Iraq. The Foreign Legion's motto is the apt **Legion Patria Nostra**— meaning "The Legion is our Homeland." It could just as well be "The Desert is our Homeland," so much time have the Legion spent there. They have fought across Africa for over 100 years, and so there are no better soldiers to teach us how to survive the cruel, arid heat of the desert.

A legionnaire takes a break during service in the Democratic Republic of Congo. This country is on the Atlantic coast of Africa.

THE WORLD'S DESERTS

Intense heat, lack of water, and a lack of food are only some of the problems you will face in the desert. But don't despair: with the French Foreign Legion as your guide, you should be able to survive, and get back to civilization.

Deserts occupy around 20 percent of the Earth's land surface. However, the idea that they are all composed of sand is wrong. There are in fact six types of desert: alkali, sand, rock, rocky plateau, and mountain. Around the world there are nine main desert areas.

Sahara Desert

The Sahara Desert is in North Africa, and the Legion have a great deal of experience here. It is an enormous desert—three million **square miles** (7,770,000 sq km). It has little vegetation, and is mainly made up of loose, shifting sand. It has areas of sandstone, limestone, and volcanic rock, salt marshes, and canyons. It is swept by hot, dry winds that cause major sandstorms. The nights are bitterly cold during the winter months, often requiring the wearing of overcoats and blankets. Rainfall is very rare in the Sahara. In an entire year the desert usually has less than five inches (12.5 cm) of rainfall. In the western and central regions, extreme temperatures range between freezing at night (32°F/0°C), and

Soldiers trek across a desert. Sand deserts are the result of rocks being broken down by extreme heat and wind over millions of years.

130°F (54.4°C) in the heat of the day. Few plants grow there, and animals include gazelle, antelope, jackal, fox, badger, and hyena.

Kalahari Desert

This desert is in the hills and mountains of South Africa, mostly in the country of Botswana. It consists of large areas of red sand and flat plains. A lot of the Kalahari is covered by a heavy growth of tough, dry trees, while to the east it is mainly sand.

Arabian Desert

The Arabian Desert extends over 500,000 square miles (1,290,000 sq km) in the Middle East. It comes close to being a complete wasteland. It has huge, continuously drifting sand dunes, and

The Sahara Desert. In June, July, and August, temperatures can reach over 120°F (48°C), the hottest time being midday.

almost no vegetation. Part of the Arabian Desert is called the Rub al-Khali. This is 250,000 square miles (650,000 sq km) in size, and is also known as the "Empty Quarter." It is the largest area of unbroken sand in the world, and it takes up one quarter of the country of Saudi Arabia.

Persian Desert

This reaches from the Persian Gulf to the Caspian Sea. Its climate is very severe; winters are bitterly cold, while temperatures in the summer are 100°F (37.8°C). The wind blows constantly from the north during the "wind of 100 days" in the summer, with speeds of up to 75 miles per hour (120 km/h).

Gobi Desert

The Gobi Desert is in China and Mongolia. It is a huge, waterless area of some 600,000 square miles (960,000 sq km) surrounded by high mountain barriers that prevent rainfall. The Gobi has almost no trees. Instead it is covered with a wiry tufted grass, long spiky thorn bushes, and gravel. There are occasional wells and shallow lakes, though the southeast of the Gobi has no water at all, and it almost never rains there. The height of the Gobi plateau ranges from 3,000 feet (914 m) in the east to 5,000 feet (152 m) in the west.

Atacama Desert

The Atacama Desert is in South America. It covers areas of Chile, Argentina, and Bolivia, and it is a desert characterized by an almost total lack of rainfall. It is completely barren and desolate, but people do live there because it contains valuable rocks and minerals, which are excavated by mining companies. The size of the Atacama is around 140,000 square miles (363,000 sq km).

The Great Basin

Situated in the United States, in Arizona, New Mexico, Nevada, Utah, Texas, Colorado, California, and northern Mexico, the Great Basin's terrain is rocky, and contains ravines, canyons, and **escarpments**. The vegetation consists of cactus and sage brush. Part of the Great Basin is the Mojave Desert in southern California, which covers an area of about 15,000 square miles (38,850 sq km).

Australian deserts

The deserts of the Australian "outback" are more or less uninhabited apart from the Aborigines, Australia's native people who are great survival experts themselves. Australian deserts have weather that can change dramatically. Sometimes there is no rain and clear hot skies for months. On other occasions they can suffer floods, cyclones, and storms. There are several main deserts within Australia. These include the Great Sandy Desert, the Great Victoria Desert, and the Simpson Desert.

Thar Desert

The Thar Desert is in northwest India and eastern Pakistan, mostly in the Indian state of Rajasthan. It is about 500 miles (800 km) long, and about 300 miles (485 km) wide. The terrain consists of sand hills mixed with shrub and rock outcrops.

What deserts are like

When we think of deserts, we tend to picture blazing hot skies. The Legion quickly teaches you that this is not always the case. Some deserts can have temperatures well below freezing. During the Gulf War, for example, soldiers from the elite SAS (U.K. Special Air Service regiment formed during World War II) found themselves surviving in a blizzard in the middle of the deserts of Iraq. Desert temperatures also vary, according to where the desert is on the planet. For example, the Gobi Desert experiences temperatures of −50°F (−10°C) in the winter. On the other hand, the Sahara Desert has recorded temperatures of up to 136°F (58°C). Yet as a general rule, deserts are hot during the day because there are few clouds to block the sunlight, but at night they become very cool when the ground releases all its heat back into the air. Because of the low

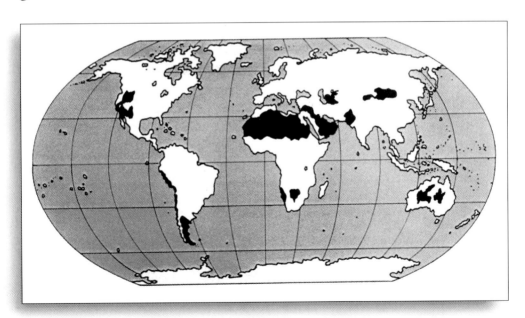

The world's desert regions shown in black in this representation of the Earth. The largest desert area is the Sahara Desert, North Africa.

cloud density, the days are abnormally bright and the nights crystal clear. Deserts can also feature very strong winds, and the lack of plants means that it is difficult to find shelter from the harsh sun.

Even though deserts differ in temperature, they all share a lack of water. Deserts have less than 10 inches (25 cm) of rainfall each year, and some deserts have no rain at all. The lack of moisture in the soil and in the atmosphere means that most of the sunlight bakes the ground, and makes it impossible for humans to grow plants there. When rains do come to the desert, they are normally very hard. As a result, flash flooding (where normally dry streambeds are filled with huge amounts of water) is very common.

Vegetation in deserts is usually scarce. What plant life there is will be specially adapted to withstand the severe conditions. Wild plants are usually found where water accumulates. Legionnaires can identify many types of desert plants because these often indicate that there is water underground. Palm trees indicate water about two to three feet (60–90 cm) under the surface; cottonwood and willow trees suggest water 10 to 12 feet (3–3.6 m) under the surface. But you need to be careful. Plants like the cactus can grow in the most barren soil, yet they do not indicate the presence of water.

Because deserts are usually flat, the winds tend to be very strong. In fact, winds in the desert can reach hurricane force, causing massive clouds of dust and sand known as dust storms. These can be very dangerous to the legionnaire. The eyes, ears, and nose are vulnerable to being filled by the swirling sand if they are not covered. Not only is this an uncomfortable, even dangerous, experience, but visibility is reduced to almost zero. It is not unusual

THE CHANGING DESERT

The desert is constantly changing shape; it is never still. Hot strong winds blow sand dunes into new shapes, something which can make navigation difficult for the survivor. If you are traveling without a map, pick permanent features to travel toward—rocks, mountains, and trees are good examples. But beware, the shifting sands can cover objects many feet high, sand dunes might disappear overnight, and the whole landscape might change if there is a sand storm.

for people in dust storms to become separated from each other even though they are only a few feet apart, such is the ferocity of a dust storm. (Legionnaires will often tie themselves together in a dust storm to avoid getting lost.)

Another special feature of the desert is **mirages**. These are the result of light being distorted when heated air rises from very hot sandy or stone surfaces. They usually occur when you are looking toward the sun, and they seem to make objects bend and ripple. A cruel effect of the mirage in the desert is to often create the illusion of water, but as you get closer the water "disappears." During your journey, you may actually "see" hills, mountains, and lakes that are actually mirages.

Other desert terrain characteristics include hillocks (a small or low hill), wadis (dry riverbeds and valleys), and oases (places where water gathers). But surprisingly, all deserts also contain at least some

Roads are a lifeline but can still be over 500 miles (800 km) long, even in small deserts like Anza-Borrego Desert State Park in California.

manmade features. As a survivor, you should look out for them: they may lead to civilization (though the distances may be great).

Roads and trails

Most road systems have existed for centuries to connect places of business or important religious shrines. In addition, there are often basic trails for caravans and nomadic tribesmen, and these often have wells or oases every 20 to 40 miles (32–64 km). However, in some areas there may be over 100 miles (160 km) between watering places.

Buildings

In the desert, most houses are thick-walled, and have small windows. The ruins of earlier civilizations often litter the deserts, even including temples and religious shrines. You can use these as temporary shelters on your journey.

Pipelines

Many deserts have long pipelines running across them. These carry water, oil, or gas great distances from one country to another. By following them, you can reach safety, and because they are often elevated above the desert floor, they can be seen from a long way away.

Even in the desert you can find evidence of civilization. Troops head for buildings like these to replenish stocks of water, medicine, and food.

Canals

In desert areas, most people live near flowing water if possible. Canals are often dug out from rivers to redirect water to crops and habitation. Following these can lead you to people as well as supply you with drinking water.

Traveling in the desert can be extremely hazardous. Because the Legion is used to marching such significant distances through the desert, they understand the rules of safety. They teach that as a

A legionnaire in World War II proudly displays his regiment's flag. His rifle is the 7.5-mm Fusil MAS36.

survivor you must consider the effect of the heat, your health, and the amount of food and water you will need to survive on your travels. Do not think that you are tougher than the climate—you are not.

Soldiers always stay covered up in the desert. This keeps them cooler than letting their skin be exposed to the sun.

The Legion's desert travel rules are as follows: Avoid the midday sun; travel only in the evening, at night, or in the early morning. Do not walk aimlessly. Try to head for a coast, a road, a path, a water source, or an inhabited location. Try to follow trails. Avoid loose sand and rough terrain; they will cause fatigue. In sandstorms, lie on your side with your back to the wind, then cover your face and sleep through the storm. (Don't worry—you won't get buried.) Seek shelter on the **leeward** side of hills. Objects always appear closer

Because we stand upright, the sun's rays hit our heads. As a result, we receive only 60 percent of the heat felt by four-legged animals.

than they really are in the desert. Therefore, multiply all your distance estimations by three.

Legionnaires reduce the risks by being expert navigators. At night they use the stars and the moon to steer their course. During the day they use a **compass** or natural landmarks. Survivors should try to follow animal trails and hope they lead to rivers or watering holes. The wind can also be used to guide you: if you know the direction in which prevailing winds are blowing, you can use them to ensure

you are going in the same direction each day. As we have learned, sandstorms can create total confusion. When the storm is over, all the landmarks you were using may be covered over entirely with sand. So when legionnaires see a storm coming, they mark their route with a tall object such as a stick or pole. When the storm is over, the stick shows them what direction they need to follow to continue their journey.

Clothing is very important in desert areas. The Legion has several items of clothing that help desert survival. Much of this clothing is copied from the native people who live in the desert. In

North Africa, for example, the Bedouin wear light-colored, loose-fitting clothing (the hooded cloak is called a "burnouse"), which covers the head and neck and gives protection against sun, wind, and sand. The cooler air trapped between the clothing and the body acts as extra protection against heat. The Legion follow the Bedouin by wearing a special hat called a **kepi**. This has a long peak to protect the eyes from the sun. It is tall to trap in lots of cool air. It also has a long piece of cloth to protect the neck from heat. All these features are very important, as extreme sunlight and heat can make you overheat, with fatal results.

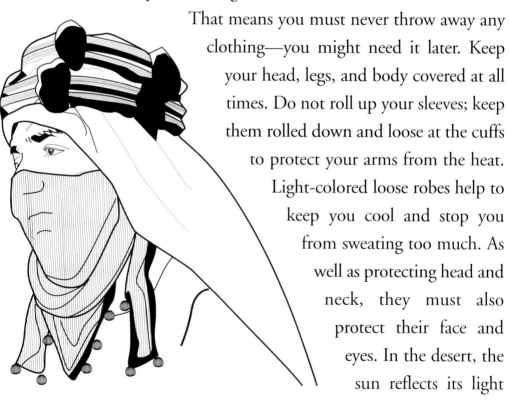

You must have protection against sunburn, heat, sand, and insects. That means you must never throw away any clothing—you might need it later. Keep your head, legs, and body covered at all times. Do not roll up your sleeves; keep them rolled down and loose at the cuffs to protect your arms from the heat. Light-colored loose robes help to keep you cool and stop you from sweating too much. As well as protecting head and neck, they must also protect their face and eyes. In the desert, the sun reflects its light

An improvised headdress should protect your head, neck, and shoulders from the heat of the sun; a face cloth keeps out the sand.

and heat off the sand. This creates a blinding glare, which can make eyesight incredibly painful, and even send the legionnaire blind if he or she does not act quickly. Wear sunglasses or goggles if you have them. If not, a large piece of cloth can be wrapped around the face, leaving only small slits—look through these. Another Legion tip to reduce glare is smearing soot from a fire on the skin below the eyes.

Many Legion battles have involved marching long distances through the desert heat. Legionnaires know that protecting the feet is vital to survival. Desert floors will be either intensely hot or intensely cold. This can cause the feet to blister and crack if they are not protected enough. The Legion offer the following tips to avoid this: Do not attempt to walk barefoot, as it is unlikely that your feet will be hard enough for long distances. If you have shoes or boots, keep sand out of them by binding cloth, bandage, or other material over the top of the footwear, and around the ankle. Check your footwear regularly and empty out any sand that is inside. This is because sand is abrasive and it can create blisters by rubbing on your skin. Also, check for scorpions and other dangerous animals when putting on footwear, especially if you have taken off your boots overnight. If your footwear is a pair of weak shoes with thin soles, you can make them stronger by putting cloth inside the shoe or rubber on the sole itself. This will make the shoes stronger, and also stop some of the heat from getting to your feet.

We now know what deserts are like, how we should move in the desert, and how we should dress to survive. Now we must let the French Foreign Legion teach us the most important lesson of all in desert survival—how to find water.

FINDING WATER

The legionnaires know a hard fact about surviving in the desert: without food, you will stay alive for about ten days—but without water, you might not last 24 hours.

In very hot conditions, the body tries to keep cool by releasing heat through the skin, and by sweating. To understand how sweating keeps you cool, think of how chilly you feel when you get out of a swimming pool. This is because the water is evaporating into the air, and taking your heat with it. Desert climates are very dangerous because you can lose more water through sweating than is available to drink. If this process goes too far, you can become dehydrated, and your blood becomes too thick to be pumped around your body by the heart. Once this happens, you can easily die. The Legion teaches three basic principles to its recruits: how to find water, how to store water, and how to stop yourself from losing too much water through sweating.

Legionnaires are taught to look for water underground. Find a dry lake or riverbed at its lowest part, and dig into the ground with a spade, stick, or rock. If you strike wet sand, stop digging at once, and let the water seep in. However, if you do not have immediate success, stop digging and find another spot; you must save your energy. To find water, you should look at the terrain closely. The

A well is essential for survival in the desert. At a temperature of 120°F (48°C) a human can, at best, live for only two days without water.

likeliest place will be at the base of a hill or canyon. Plants growing from canyon walls are a good indicator that there is water present. Reeds, grass, willows, cottonwoods, and palm trees usually mark permanent water sources.

The Bushman of the Kalahari Desert uses the following method for finding water. He finds the deepest part of an old, dry stream, then digs down until he finds moist sand. He takes a tube almost five feet (1.5 m) long, made from the stem of a bush with a soft

A dry riverbed is, strangely, one of the best places to find water, which can be found by digging five feet (1.5 m) into the soil.

core, and winds four inches (10 cm) of dry grass lightly around one end. The Bushman then inserts the tube into the hole, and packs the sand around it, stamping down the sand with his feet. He sucks on the tube hard for about two minutes, and eventually water comes into his mouth.

Water can also be found in moist sand or mud. Put the sand or mud into a cloth, and wring it out into a container. During the rainy season, ensure that any rain is caught by laying out a plastic bag with a stone in the middle so that water flows into the center.

Legionnaires train themselves to live off the land, and desert plants can be valuable water sources. These are the main types of plants that can give you a good drink:

Cactus

If you cut off the top of a barrel cactus and squeeze the pulp you find inside, water will trickle out.

Date palms

Cut at a lower branch near the base of the tree, and liquid should ooze from the cut.

Agave plants take 8–12 years to grow. The flowers and flower buds can be cooked and eaten.

Baobab tree

Its large trunk collects water when it has been raining.

A large cactus from the North American deserts can produce over two pints (1 liter) of drinkable, water-rich sap when cut open.

Prickly pears

Their fruit and earlike lobes both contain water.

Saxaul

This is a large shrub or tree. It has a spongy bark containing water. If you press hard large amounts of the bark, water will come out.

Roots

Some trees have roots lying near the surface. These can be cut and sucked to provide moisture.

If you are lucky enough to find a pool of open water, beware. Some water in the desert can be poisonous, particularly lakes. Signs of poisonous water are: dead animals lying around; the water smells bad; foam or bubbles are on the surface of the water; or there are no fresh and healthy plants nearby. In these circumstances, it is best not to drink the water at all.

When you do find water, make it safe to drink by purifying it. The simplest way to do this is to first pour the water through a piece of cloth (this removes any large pieces of dirt), and then boil it over a fire for 10 minutes (boiling kills germs). After that, put in **purification tablets**. These are chemicals that make water safe to drink, and all legionnaires in the desert carry them. Water from plants, trees, shrubs, or dew rain will not need purifying.

As well as finding water sources, legionnaires are also trained to make their own water. Dew may form at night in the cooler months, and making a **solar still** is an effective way of catching it

Prickly pears originated in North America, but they have now spread to deserts throughout the world. The fruit can be peeled and eaten.

and turning it into a drink. You should dig a hole three feet (90 cm) across and two feet (60 cm) deep. Dig a drainage hole in the middle of the main hole, and put a container in it, then place a plastic sheet over the hole, and secure it with sand, dirt, or rocks. Place a rock in the center of the sheet. The sun raises the overall temperature of the air and soil in the hole to produce vapor. Water then condenses on the underside of the plastic sheet and runs down into the container.

Once you have water, you have to make sure that you do not sweat it all away as soon as you have drunk it. In the desert, water definitely comes before food. If you have food but little or no water, eat only small amounts until you find a fresh supply of water, because digesting food uses up large amounts of the body's fluids. If water is available, work out a sensible ration. Then drink at least enough to make you think straight. This will make it easier to plan how to locate other sources of water.

In extreme desert heat, you can lose up to 4 pints (1.5 liters) of the body's water through sweating each hour. If you lose more water than you are drinking, this could eventually lead to serious illness or death. French Foreign Legionnaires use the following techniques to conserve water:

- If you stay fully clothed, you will sweat a lot less.
- Do not use water for washing unless you have plenty of it.

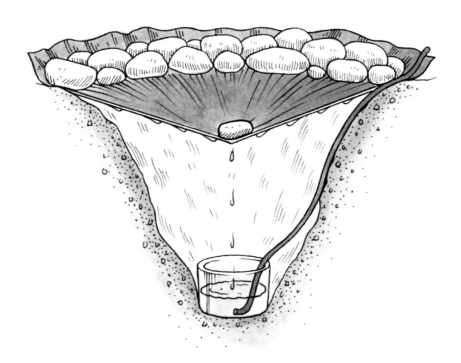

The solar still has a tube that runs down into the water container. The survivor can drink without having to take the still apart.

- Do not rush around, since this will make you sweat more.
- Drink water in small sips, not gulps. If water supplies are very low, use it only to moisten your lips.
- Keep small pebbles in your mouth or chew grass to relieve thirst.
- Use salt only with water, and only if you have a regular supply of water.

Our bodies are actually 75 percent water. This water keeps us at the right temperature of about 100°F (38°C).

SIGNS OF WATER

The soldiers of the French Foreign Legion have become experts at finding water in the barren desert. After all, it can be a matter of life and death. The following are some of the signs they look out for:

• Swarming insects; watch in particular for bees or columns of ants.
• Lots of plants; vegetation is at its best when there is water nearby.
• Animals; grazing animals need water at dusk and dawn, though meat-eaters get liquid from their prey so they may not be heading for a water source.
• Large clumps of lush grass.
• Springwater seeping through rocks and mud.
• Birds; these might gather around water, but bear in mind that some birds fly long distances to get to water.

• If you have the chance to build a shelter, stay inside it during the hottest part of the day.
• Do not talk, and breathe through the nose not the mouth.

By following the Legion's guidelines, you should find enough water to keep you alive in even the most hostile deserts. But as well as water, you will also need food.

FINDING FOOD

Deserts might seem to offer little or no food. Yet the Legion soldiers can find food sources in the most difficult places on earth. With their specialized training they know how and where to find a variety of plants and animals.

One of the biggest rules of desert survival is: Do not eat unless you have water. Legion training says that if you can get only one pint (0.473 liters) of water a day, you should not eat at all. However, if you do have enough water, this is what the Legion recommends you eat.

Plants

The types of plant food available vary according to the desert. However, some plants are fairly common, and a legionnaire will be able to identify the following types.

Carob

Appearance: has shiny, evergreen leaves paired in groups of two or three to a stem. *Edible parts*: its small red flowers have leathery seed pods. These contain a sweet, nutritious pulp that can be eaten raw. In addition, the hard brown seeds can be ground up with a stone and cooked as oatmeal.

Troops need up to a third more calories in cold climates than in hot ones, since extra energy is needed in the cold to generate body heat.

Edible carob plants grow in deserts from Europe to India. Another name given to this plant is St. John's Bread.

Acacias

Appearance: thorny, medium-sized trees with very small leaves. Their white, pink, or yellow flowers form small round flowerheads. *Edible parts*: use the roots for water; the seeds can be roasted, and the young leaves and shoots boiled.

Baobabs

Appearance: large trees with huge, heavily swollen trunks. These trunks can be up to 30 feet (9 m) in diameter. *Edible parts*: cut into the roots for water. The fruits and seeds can be eaten raw. The tender young leaves should be boiled.

Date palms

Appearance: tall, slender palms with a tuft of leaves at the top. They can be up to 16 feet (4.8 m) long. *Edible parts*: the fruits and growing tip of the palm can be eaten raw; the sap from the trunk is rich in sugar, and can be boiled down.

Mescals

Appearance: thick, leathery, spiky leaves, out of which grows a very long flower stalk. *Edible parts*: the stalk is edible when cooked.

Trees such as the acacia (pictured here) are a good source of water, since desert plants often store water in their roots.

Wild gourds

Appearance: the plant resembles a vine, with orange-sized fruits.
Edible parts: you can boil the unripe fruit to make it more edible.
Cook young leaves, roast the seeds, and chew the stems and shoots
for their water.

Carrion flowers

Appearance: large plants with succulent stems that branch off into
leaves like fat spines. They have star-shaped flowers covered in thick,

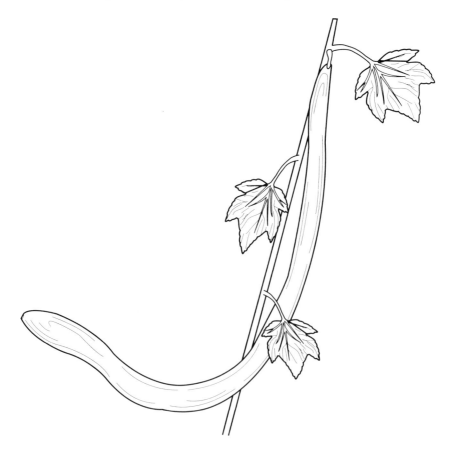

**Wild gourds occur in several of the world's largest deserts, including
the Kalahari, the Sahara, and also the deserts of India.**

shaggy hairs. The flowers give off a stench of rotting meat, which gives them their name. *Edible parts*: you can tap the stems for water.

Prickly pears

Appearance: have thick, padlike leaves, yellow or red flowers, and egg-shaped pulpy fruits. *Edible parts*: the peeled fruits can be eaten raw, the pads must be cooked. (Cut away the spines.) Roast the seeds for flour, and tap the stems for water.

Desert grasses

All desert grasses are edible. The best part is the whitish tender end that shows when the grass stalk is pulled from the ground; you can also eat grass seeds. Flowers that have milky or colored sap are poisonous.

Animals

Insects can be one of the easiest types of animal to eat in the desert. Most people don't like the thought of eating insects, but they can make a tasty meal. However, avoid caterpillars, because a few species are poisonous, and stay clear of centipedes and scorpions.

The Foreign Legion has various guidelines for trapping and eating insects. You can attract insects to you at night with a small light, or crawling insects can be gathered by lifting up stones. The **larvae** of ants make particularly good eating. Brush ants from the undersides of stones into a container of water, and the larvae will float to the top. If eating grasshoppers or crickets, always remove the wings and legs before eating. Grasshoppers should always be cooked.

You need many insects to make a meal, so it is good if you can catch and eat bigger animals. Most desert animals—mammals, birds, reptiles, and insects—are edible. You may have to lay traps for the larger animals and birds. However, keep a watch for owls, hawks, vultures, and foxes, which often gather around freshly killed animals. You need the food just as much as them so chase them away, and take the meat for yourself.

Rabbits and birds can be trapped by nets and snares, but rabbits can be smoked out of their holes by building a fire at the entrance. Be ready to club them when they come out. Snakes make a tasty meal, but remember they may be poisonous. You will often find them sunning themselves on rocks and ledges when the sun is not too hot. (When the sun is hottest, they will stay in shaded areas.) They are most active during the early morning or early evening. Only the nonpoisonous varieties should be approached, but even then make sure you are armed with a forked stick and club. Lizards can also be eaten. Look for them under flat stones

Though insects look unappetizing, they actually provide more nutrients per ounce (25 g) than vegetables.

at dawn, before the sun has warmed the air, and kill them by throwing stones at them or using a catapult. Reptiles in general are another good source of protein, but beware of the poisonous varieties, which may lurk in shaded areas, caves, and caverns.

Like the reptiles, most desert mammals are largely nocturnal. Rodents should be snared with a loop snare when they emerge from their holes at dusk or dawn. Animals like the Arabian oryx will require a great deal of skill with a spear or a good shot with a rifle to bring it down. In the Gobi Desert, herds of antelope can be found. Partridge, quail, and bustard frequent water sources in the deserts of Iran and Iraq. When looking for animals, keep an eye out for obvious signs such as droppings, tracks, trails, and feeding areas.

The oryx will make a tasty meal, but beware—its three-foot (90-cm) horns are very dangerous.

Cooking

Legion soldiers are trained not just to catch food but also to cook it. They use the materials on hand,

and turn raw meat into a tasty meal. They teach the following cooking methods.

Boiling

Make a boiling pot by scooping a hole in hard ground, lining it with leaves or other waterproof material, filling it with water, and then dropping red-hot coals from the fire into it. In mountainous deserts, you can find rocks with holes in them made by erosion. You can use them as boiling pots; heat them on the fire before filling them with water. Large plant leaves can be bent into containers to hold water. (They will not burn while being held over a flame as long as you keep them filled with water.) Barrel cacti can also be used as containers; mash the pulp inside them and scoop it out, then use the shells for cooking.

LEGIONNAIRE TIPS ON EATING INSECTS

- Be careful when hunting for insects; their hiding places may also conceal scorpions, spiders, and snakes.
- Do not eat insects that have fed on manure; they carry disease and infection.
- Cook ants for at least six minutes to kill any poisons they might be carrying.
- Do not eat brightly colored insects; they are poisonous.
- Do not collect grubs found on the underside of leaves; they give out poisonous fluids.

Frying

A skillet (frying pan) can be made from desert rocks. Find a flat and narrow rock, then prop it up with other rocks and build a fire underneath it. (Make sure you wipe off all the grit and dirt before you heat it.) The rock will heat up, letting you fry meat or eggs on it.

Roasting

Make sure that you have a good bed of glowing coals, then place your meat on a green stick and hold it near the embers.

Soldiers can easily make kebabs in the desert as long as they have a source of fire and meat. First, prepare a bed of hot, glowing embers. Then cut your meat into small cubes all the same size, and spear each one with a stick that has a sharpened end. Roast each meat cube evenly over the hot coals. (Make sure they do not slip off the sticks.)

Mud baking

This is an excellent way of cooking small animals. First, clean the carcass by removing the head, feet, and tail. Leave the skin or feathers on the animal. Cover the carcass completely with mud or clay at least one inch (2.5 cm) thick, then place in a large fire and cover with coals. The animal may take up to an hour to cook, depending on its size. When the clay is hard and bricklike, remove it from the fire and break it open. When you do this, the feathers or skin will break away at the same time, leaving a ready meal.

Broiling

Dig a hole larger and wider than the animal to be cooked, about one to three feet (30–90 cm) deep. Build a fire at the bottom of it, and wait until it is hot. Then spread green twigs over the top of the hole, and place the meat on top of them. You can put small stones in the fire to radiate the heat.

Earth baking

Dig a hole two feet (60 cm) wide and two feet (60 cm) deep. Gather some wood, and make a criss-cross pattern over the hole, putting one layer of sticks in one direction and one layer in another. Then lay a number of medium-sized stones on top of the sticks. Start a fire in the hole and let it burn until the stones turn white and fall into the hole. Arrange the stones in the hole and shovel out any pieces of burning wood, then cover the stones with a lot of green leaves that have been moistened with water, and throw the food to be cooked on top. Cover the food with another batch of leaves, and then cover the hole with earth to ensure no steam escapes. After about two hours, the food will be cooked. This is an excellent method of cooking but requires speed when you are arranging the stones to ensure they do not cool.

Once the techniques of finding food are mastered, then even the desert can yield plenty to eat. These techniques take a lot of practice, but the legionnaires are experts because they have to be. Without these techniques, the legionnaires would not have gained their reputation as expert desert warriors. Paying attention to the lessons they teach can literally be a matter of life and death.

Cooking kills bacteria and parasites living in food, and a hot meal also serves to raise your spirits. High morale is crucial to survival.

SHELTER

The desert sun is cruel. A legionnaire in the desert will need to make a shelter quickly if he or she is not to become sunburned, dehydrated, or drop dead.

Shelter is extremely important in the desert. Shelter protects you from heat during the day, and keeps you warm during the intense cold of the night. Try to copy the Legion when it comes to making shelters. They can create shelters out of almost nothing. Though these might not be comfortable, they dramatically increase the chances of surviving in the desert.

The weather can play a key part in determining the location and type of shelter a legionnaire builds. In warm areas, make shelters in places open to breezes, but beware of exposing a shelter to blowing sand or dust, both of which can cause injury and damage. Insects can also be a problem around a camp. If you build your shelter where there is a breeze or steady wind, you can reduce the number of insects that will pester you. Avoid building a shelter near standing water; it attracts mosquitoes, bees, wasps, and hornets. Do not erect a shelter on or near an ant hill, unless you want a never-ending succession of bites and stings. When you are building your shelter, look above you. The tree you are under may contain a bees' or hornets' nest, which you will obviously want to avoid. In addition,

Caves are very common in rocky desert areas. They are formed either by desert winds or prehistoric rivers which have now dried up.

A simple sun shelter like this is used by the Legion. Do not place your shelter in a valley, as desert rains can quickly raise water levels.

watch out for dead wood in trees above you. Your shelter might be firmly in place at that moment, but in the next storm or high wind it could come crashing down on you and your shelter.

Natural shelters can be scarce in the desert, and limited to the shade of cliffs and the shadow sides of hills, dunes, or rock formations. Caves are a good shelter in rocky areas, but you will have to look carefully for them because they are small and easy to miss. Caves are cool, and they may contain water. However, they can also contain animals: rats, mice, snakes, and rabbits. Although these are all food sources, sensible survivors will be aware of the dangers of bites and stings. Therefore, stay near the entrance.

In flat, open deserts, natural shelters are harder to find. However, gather together tumbleweeds or other plants and mat them together to make into a shelter. In some deserts, the sand two feet (50 cm) below the surface can be as much as 20 or 30 degrees cooler than the air above it. Dig into the sand, and construct a trench three feet (90 cm) deep dug in a north–south direction to provide shade during the day. Cover it to provide more protection. When building your shelter, you must bear in mind three other Legion lessons:

• Watch the weather. If a storm is threatening, avoid gullies, washes, or areas with little vegetation. They are prone to floods and high winds.

This desert shelter was built by Allied troops during the Gulf War. Some troops would drink over 55 pints (30 liters) of water each day!

- Poisonous snakes, centipedes, and scorpions may be hiding in brush or under rocks
- Do not make camp at the base of steep slopes or in areas where you run the risk of floods, rockfalls, or heavy winds.

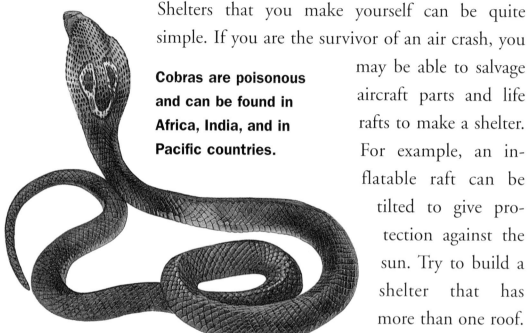

Cobras are poisonous and can be found in Africa, India, and in Pacific countries.

Shelters that you make yourself can be quite simple. If you are the survivor of an air crash, you may be able to salvage aircraft parts and life rafts to make a shelter. For example, an inflatable raft can be tilted to give protection against the sun. Try to build a shelter that has more than one roof. The air gap between two roofs reduces the temperature inside the shelter. You should place the floor of the shelter about 18 inches (45 cm) above or below the desert surface to increase the cooling effect. Try to use a white material as the outer layer of the shelter. The sides of the shelter should be movable to protect you during cold and windy periods, and to offer ventilation in the extreme heat.

Knowing when and where to build desert shelters can save you a lot of time and energy. Follow the advice of the French Foreign Legion. Build shelters during the early morning, late evening, or at night. It is less physically tiring because it is cooler at these times. It is better to build a full shelter in the morning or evening, and to improvise temporary shelter during the heat of the day. Try to build a shelter near fuel (wood) and water if possible. Build shelters away from rocks, which store up heat during the day. You may wish to move to rocky areas during the night, however, to take advantage of the warmth.

The type of shelter you choose will depend on your circumstances, and the material you have available. If you are near a crashed

Soldiers have to fight from their shelters. Here a soldier mans a 7.62-mm caliber General Purpose Machine Gun (GPMG).

plane, for example, it is a good idea to build a shelter near the aircraft, because rescuers will be able to spot you more easily. Do not shelter inside the airplane in the desert since it is likely to be too hot.

One of the most basic shelters is constructed of rocks with a roof made of canvas or other material. Stretch the material from the top of the rocks to the ground, weighing down each end with stones, sand, or other weights. The same type of shelter can be used on a sand dune or mound of sand. For either kind of shelter, two layers of material are better than one. Leave a gap of about 16 inches (40 cm) between them, and place some light-colored material on the outside to reflect the sun's rays.

Another type of shelter Legion soldiers use is an underground shelter. This shelter will take more time to make, and should be

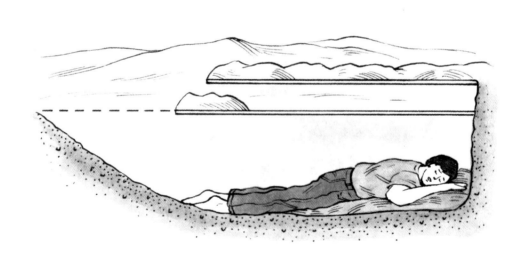

Underground shelters can be incredibly cool because the ground above soaks up the heat of the sun.

MAKE THE MOST OF CAVES

Natural shelters can be quite hard to come by in desert areas, but caves make excellent shelters. It is essential to find shelter in order to be protected, not only from the heat of the sun in the day but also the cold of night. If you take shelter in a cave in a cliff or rocky outcrop, you can increase its warmth at night by making a windbreak over the entrance. You can use stones, rocks, or earth. If you light a fire in the cave, light it at the back or the smoke will blow around and choke you.

made when the temperature is lower. Find a depression in the ground, a suitable area between rocks, or dig a trench up to 25 inches (62.5 cm) deep. Make sure that you will be able to lie in the sunken area comfortably and store any equipment you may have. Place your material over the area. If you have dug a trench, pile the sand around three sides of it to anchor the material, and leave an entrance. If you have enough material, place a second layer over the first, with a gap of about 18 inches (45 cm). You can also make a shelter with four open sides. This is like the underground shelter but is constructed with all sides open, and anchored at the four corners of the material.

A good shelter is one of the best methods for protecting yourself from the daytime sun of the desert. With a little thought, the most basic of materials, and the legionnaires' expertise, you can protect yourself from the worst of the desert heat.

DANGERS

Survival in the desert is tough. Legionnaires not only have to fight in the desert, they also have to know what natural dangers surround them.

The main threat to anyone surviving in the desert is the heat, but also the dangerous animals and plants that can injure or poison you. However, the Legion soldiers can teach you to avoid all these things and stay safe.

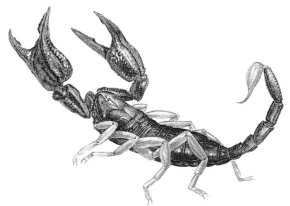

Scorpions live across the world— one is even found at high altitude in the Andes Mountains of Peru.

Some of the first dangers that face you are from plants and insects. Most desert plants are protected by sharp thorns or spines. The spines have tiny hooks on them that will stick to your skin or clothing if you touch them. Do not go near them. If you do touch them, try to wash your skin. Many insects are also aggressive. Avoid ant nests. (They look like big mounds of soil.) If you are bitten, put wet mud on the bite—this will soothe any redness, and reduce the pain. Centipedes should also be avoided; their bites can be very

Aiming a gun in the desert is difficult because of the shimmering heat haze, caused by water evaporating from the ground.

Black widow spiders can be found in all four deserts of the southwestern United States. A similar brown widow also lives in Texas.

painful and the effects can last up to two weeks. They hide under rocks during the day, and move at night.

Scorpions stay under rocks during the day, and move around at night, often into sleeping bags or boots. Shake out your boots in the morning to check if there are any scorpions inside as their bite can be deadly. Spider bites are also common in the wild. If you are bitten, you will have to endure pain, nausea, dizziness, and difficulty in breathing for a few days. It is far better to avoid spiders. Do not tease or try to capture them. You may encounter the following spiders in desert regions.

Black widow

Appearance: small, dark, and has a red, yellow, or white marking on the body. *Bite symptoms*: severe pain, sweating, shivering, and weakness. Can disable a victim for up to a week.

Fiddleback

Appearance: has a violin shape on the back of the head. *Bite symptoms*: fever, chills, vomiting, pain in your joints, and spots on the skin.

Tarantula

Appearance: large and hairy. *Bite symptoms*: some pain, but the poison is fairly mild.

Much more serious than spider bites are bites from poisonous snakes. Venomous snakes found in desert areas include the cobra, viper, and rattlesnake. Your best protection against snake bites is to wear protective clothing—most bites are below the knee or on the hand or forearm. Do not put your hands into places you cannot see, do not try to catch a snake unless you are certain you can kill it, and always wear boots. Be careful where you tread.

When a spider is frightened, it raises its front legs and fangs in the air. Walk away or, if you are trapped, give the spider a stick to bite.

Legion soldiers are trained to recognize snakes from all corners of the world.

North and South America
Mojave rattlesnake
Deadly poisonous. Found in the Mojave Desert, California, Nevada, Arizona, Texas, and Mexico. Pale or sandy in color. Diamond-shaped marks next to light-colored scales, and bands around the tail. *Length*: average 30 inches (75 cm); maximum four feet (1.2 m).

Western diamondback rattlesnake
Dangerously poisonous. Found in Arizona, southeastern California, New Mexico, Oklahoma, and Texas. Light, yellowish-brown color with darker brown diamond-shaped markings. The tail has thick black and white bands. *Length*: average five feet (1.5 m); maximum six and a half feet (2 m).

Africa and Asia
Boomslang
Deadly poisonous. Found in Africa beneath the Sahara. Green or brown in color. *Length*: average two feet (60 cm); maximum five feet (1.5 m).

Egyptian cobra
Deadly poisonous. Found in Africa, Iraq, Syria, and Saudi Arabia. Black, yellow, or dark brown with brown crossbands. The head

is sometimes black. *Length*: average five feet (1.5 m); maximum eight feet (2.5 m).

Horned desert viper

Dangerously poisonous. Found in Africa, Arabian Peninsula, Iran, and Iraq. Pale yellowish brown in color, with a scale over each eye. *Length*: average 18 inches (45 cm); maximum 30 inches (75 cm).

McMahon's viper

Dangerously poisonous. Found in Pakistan and Afghanistan. Sandy yellowish brown in color with dark brown spots on body. Broad nose. *Length*: average 18 inches (45 cm); maximum three feet (90 cm).

Palestinian viper

Dangerously poisonous. Found in Israel, Lebanon, Jordan, Syria, and Turkey. Zigzag mark on the back, and green to brown in color.

Snakes blend into the desert floor, so are difficult to spot. If you have no choice but to kill one, hit it sharply on the head with a long stick.

Puff adder

Dangerously poisonous. Found in Africa, Israel, Jordan, Iraq, and Saudi Arabia. Yellowy, light brown, or orange, with dark brown or black bars. *Length*: average four feet (1.2 m); maximum six feet (1.8 m).

Sand viper

Dangerously poisonous. Found in central Africa, Algeria, Chad, Egypt, Nigeria, Northern Sahara, and Sudan. Pale with three rows of dark brown spots. *Length*: average 18 inches (45 cm); maximum two feet (60 cm).

Saw-scaled viper

Dangerously poisonous. Found in Africa, Algeria, Asia, India, Iran, Israel, Jordan, Egypt, Pakistan, Saudi Arabia, Sri Lanka. Light yellowish brown in color with shades of brown, red, or gray. The sides are a lighter color. Usually two dark stripes on the head. *Length*: average 18 inches (45 cm); maximum two feet (60 cm).

SNAKES AT NIGHT

At night, when the desert temperature drops, snakes look for any warmth they can find. If you are sleeping in the desert in a sleeping bag, and you find a snake has joined you, keep very still and slowly lift up the neck of the sleeping bag. The cold rush of air should send the snake slithering off to find somewhere else.

Australasia

Death adder

Deadly poisonous. Found in Australia, New Guinea, and the Moluccas. Color varies between red, yellow, and brown, with dark brown crossbands. Tail black at the end. *Length*: average 18 inches (45 cm); maximum three feet (90 cm).

Taipan

Deadly poisonous. It is found in Northern Australia and southern New Guinea. The taipan is olive or dark brown in color, with

The crossbow is a good silent hunting weapon. The first recorded use of a crossbow was in 341 B.C. at the battle of Ma-Ling in China.

darker brown head. *Length*: average six feet (1.8 m); maximum 12 feet (3.6 m).

Tiger snake

Dangerously poisonous. Found in Australia, Bass Strait Islands, Tasmania, and New Guinea. Olive or dark brown in color, with yellow or olive belly, and crossbands. The species in Tasmania is black. *Length*: average four feet (1.2 m); maximum six feet (1.8 m).

It is not only snakes and spiders that are poisonous. Lizards can be as well. Both the gila monster and beaded lizard (both around 18 in/45 cm long) are poisonous. The gila monster has a large rounded head, thick chunky body, short stumpy tail, and is brightly patterned yellow. The beaded lizard is darker and larger with a slender tail. Both these creatures are docile, and will run away from you if you leave them alone. Do not tease or corner them; their bite is very poisonous.

Nonpoisonous animal bites can be just as serious as those from poisonous animals. Mammals can carry the disease **rabies**, one of the most deadly illnesses on the planet. If you are bitten, wash the bite area with soap and water immediately, and apply disinfectant (if you have it). If a member of your party has rabies and is in the advanced stage, isolate the victim, and tie him or her down. Unfortunately, the person will certainly die—do not touch the body after death. Animals in the advanced stage of rabies, especially dogs, will be violent, will stagger, and foam at the mouth. If you are the victim of an unprovoked animal attack, you have good reason to think that the animal has rabies. Hospital treatment for rabies must be started within one or two days to be effective.

Thankfully, most of the dangers from animals in the desert can be avoided simply by not going near the creatures. However, Legion soldiers spend a lot of time learning what these creatures look like. You should do the same if you are heading for any desert region.

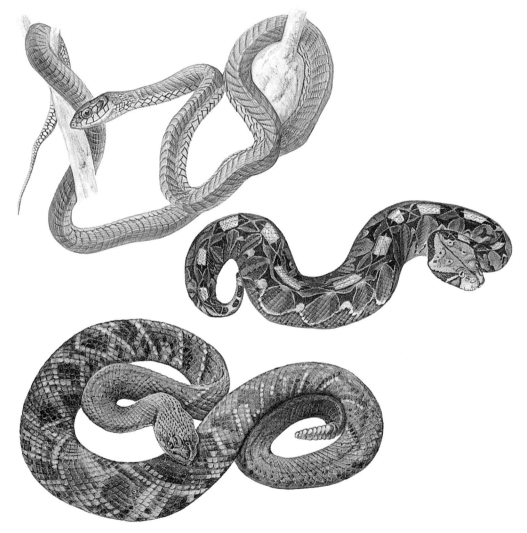

Most snakes, like the the boomslang (top), gaboon viper (middle), and Mexican rattlesnake (bottom), will not attack unless provoked.

FIRST AID

Even the toughest legionnaires can be made ill by the heat of the desert. Thankfully, they know the essential first aid to make themselves better and carry on surviving.

Because they spend so much time in the desert, legionnaires must know how to treat the illnesses and injuries that can occur there. The illnesses they face most are those connected to the heat of the desert sun.

Heat cramps are caused when too much salt in the body is lost through sweating. When this happens, pains are felt in the muscles, particularly in the abdomen, arms, and legs. The symptoms are shallow breathing, vomiting, and dizziness. Move the patient into shade, and provide water with salt dissolved in it. **Heat exhaustion** is more serious. People with heat exhaustion feel fatigue, dizziness, or nausea. They may have a temperature above normal, and will sweat heavily. Their skin will be moist and clammy and they will have a weak pulse. First aid involves cooling them down—get them into the shade, and fan them. Also give them small sips of water. These simple treatments should help them quickly feel better.

Heatstroke is the most serious condition. It is caused when people sweat out too much of their body fluid. Humans will die after losing 12 to 13 percent of their weight as body water. When

During the Gulf War the medical services were kept busy with all sorts of injuries, including animal bites and heat exhaustion.

the body dries out, the blood becomes very thick and cannot circulate around the body properly. Death can follow quite rapidly if this happens.

The symptoms of heatstroke are hot, dry skin; no sweat; a red face and feverishness; a high temperature with a rapid, strong pulse; severe headaches; and frequent vomiting. The victim may become unconscious. The body temperature must be lowered as soon as possible. The legionnaires have an excellent method for doing just that. Lay the victim in the shade, with the head and shoulders slightly raised. Remove the outer clothes, wet the inner clothes, and fan the patient. If no water is available, dig a trench in the sand and

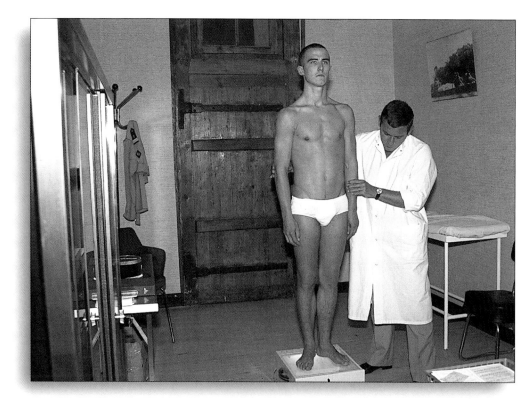

A Legion medical exam. A soldier heading for the desert will have vaccinations for smallpox, cholera, yellow fever, hepatitis, and typhoid.

A modern military field hospital. In Vietnam, an injured soldier would be on the operating table only 35 minutes after being wounded.

place the victim in the bottom. When the patient is conscious again, provide water with salt added.

The best way to prevent these illnesses is to stop **dehydration**— when the body loses too much fluid. Be careful your body does not dehydrate. In very high, dry temperatures you might not notice how much you are sweating because it evaporates quickly. You must try to keep sweat on the skin to keep you cool—avoid direct sunlight on the skin, and stay clothed. Remember, thirst is not always an accurate warning of dehydration. Keep up your fluid intake.

In the desert you are also vulnerable to various diseases carried by insects. You must try to prevent these illnesses through keeping clean. Try not to get cuts and scratches; in the desert they can become infected very easily. Clean all cooking and eating utensils and protect food and utensils from flies. Dispose garbage and human waste carefully. Do not expose your skin to the weather or to flies. Try to wash your feet and body daily. Change your socks regularly. You must check yourself for signs of any injury, and cover up any wounds with a bandage.

Apart from these dangerous illnesses, sunburn is one of the most common injuries for poorly trained people in the desert. It does not occur among legionnaires. Even in the hottest climates, legionnaires make sure that their vulnerable skin is well covered, using long-sleeved shirts, hats, and pants.

Sunburn tends to be more serious for people with light-colored skin. It ranges from a light redness and tenderness of the skin to a deep red and blistered surface.

A Legion soldier stands to attention. His weapon is the FAMAS rifle, an effective weapon, which fires the same bullet as the U.S. M16.

Do not burst any blisters but treat by applying what are known as "cold compresses" for around ten minutes. These are simply pieces of water-soaked material pressed onto the wound and soaked regularly to keep it chilled. Also give the victim cold water to drink. Most important, get the person into shelter or, if your have to keep moving, covered up with clothing.

Most of the injuries from the sun can easily be prevented. The Legion takes the power of the sun very seriously, and so should anyone who is attempting to survive the desert heat.

Give a person suffering from heat exhaustion regular sips of water.
If a person suffers from 20 percent fluid loss, they will be very ill.

When treating a casualty, you must get them into shade. Adults can sweat at least one pint (0.4 liter) of water per hour in a hot climate.

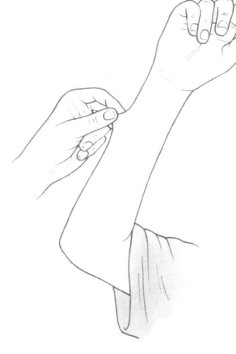

To see if someone is dehydrated, pinch the skin, then let go. If it goes back slowly, they are probably dehydrated. The patient should be given water as quickly as possible so their body can rehydrate. Dehydration can be a killer if left untreated for too long.

CHECKING A PULSE

If someone is suffering from excessive exposure to heat, their pulse may be weak. Members of the elite forces check the pulse by following this procedure: Place three fingers on the patient's wrist, about a half inch (1 cm) in from the little finger side. You should feel the pulse beating. Another place you can find the pulse is just beneath the jaw, either side of the windpipe. If you have trouble finding a pulse, and the person seems very ill, then quick medical attention needs to be sought before they get worse.

NAVIGATION

Some deserts seem almost featureless. Trying to find your way across this landscape can be extremely challenging. Yet the Legion has ways to ensure they keep going in the right direction.

As elite soldiers, the men of the Legion must know where they are at all times. In the desert this can be difficult. Without a compass, desert navigation is awkward since there are few features to use as landmarks. However, there are a few simple Legion techniques you can follow to help you navigate.

One method of navigating is to follow objects in direct line with each other, and as far apart as possible. Before one object is reached, a third should be chosen in direct line with the second, and so on. Another method is by using the stars. The desert nights will normally be clear. This allows identification of the **Southern Cross**, which indicates true south, and the North Star, which points to the north. These can be very useful because nighttime is one of the best times for traveling, since the temperatures are cool and good for saving your energy.

Because the sun is usually so strong in the desert, shadows can be an excellent method of finding out the direction in which you are heading. The Legion has a tried-and-tested method of finding out where they are using just a stick and the shadow of the sun. Place a

Compass and binoculars are two of the best navigation tools for the desert. A compass needle always points to "magnetic north."

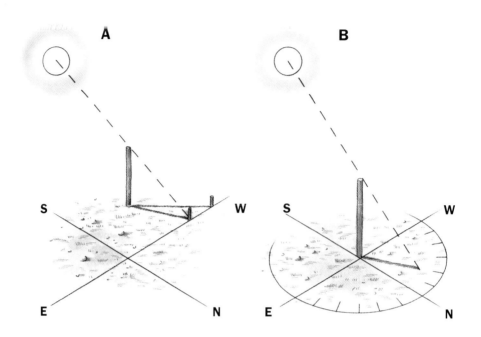

The shadow stick method of direction finding is ideal for the desert because of the bright sunshine.

stick or branch in a level piece of ground at the intersection of the east–west line and north–south line (shown in Diagram B). Regardless of where you are in the world, the west part of the east–west line will always show 0600 hours at sunrise, and the east part of the line will always show 1800 hours at sunset (Diagram A). The north–south line is used as the noon line and the shadow cast by the stick becomes the hour hand. The shadow may move clockwise or counterclockwise, depending on your location and the time of year, but this does not alter your manner of reading the shadow clock.

Another difficulty in the desert can be assessing distances. The clear atmosphere makes objects appear closer than they really are. To help you, multiply what you estimate the distance to be by sight by three. It will also be necessary to use a more accurate method of working out distances. A good method of estimating a distance is to measure it through the number of paces taken. The average stride of a man is 30 inches (75 cm), which is 25 feet (7.5 m) every 10 steps. It is useful to know the length of your own stride, and to practice measuring distances in this way, before embarking on an expedition. Another method of estimating distance is by using a watch, working on the

Sand deserts are confusing landscapes, because they are constantly changing as the wind blows the sand around.

knowledge that the average person walks about two and a half miles (4 km) per hour. Take care to adjust for difficult terrain, such as deep sand, when you will walk much more slowly.

The Global Positioning System is an advanced navigational tool. It uses satellites orbiting the earth to give an exact position reading.

One technique that can help you to navigate is to make your own maps. This technique is used by the Legion as well as by units such as the Green Berets. All you need is paper, something to write with, and a keen eye. First, find a high vantage point and look out over the terrain in front of you. Then start to draw what you see in front of you as if you were looking straight down. Make a general map with blank patches, and then fill it in as you gain more information from other vantage points. Mark on your map anything that stands out—trees, strange rocks, hills, the direction of ridges, and riverbeds. You can also use your map to mark your traps and areas where food and fuel can be found. This can be very helpful to your fellow survivors.

By making maps, using the stars and sun, and also using traditional compasses, you should have a clear idea where you are going in the desert. The Legion teaches you that you should not do anything in the desert without knowing why you are doing it. The Legion has learned the hard way that any mistakes can cost you your life. That's why they have become such experts.

SUNRISE AND SUNSET

One of the simplest ways to navigate in the desert, and a method often used by legionnaires, is to remember that the sun rises in the east and sets in the west. So as the sun comes up, or as it is setting, plot the course you intend to take. Remember, however, that you might have to use different methods during the other parts of day.

GLOSSARY

ALN The soldiers who fought against the French during the war in Algeria in the 1960s.

Compass A device with a needle that always points to the north.

Dehydration An illness that occurs when someone loses more of their body's water than they take in through drink.

Equator The imaginary line that runs around the middle of the Earth where the sun is at its hottest.

Escarpments Long, steep slopes at the edge of a plateau.

Headdress A piece of material used to cover the head and neck, to protect them from the rays of the sun.

Heat exhaustion A very dangerous condition that occurs when the victim is so hot their body cannot cope, and they become very ill.

Indochina A country in Southeast Asia, which was a French colony for many years, and where the Foreign Legion fought the communist Viet Minh guerrillas.

Kepi The hat worn by the French Foreign Legion. It is tall and round with a long peak to keep the sun out of the eyes.

Larvae The active immature form of an insect—for example, caterpillars or grubs.

Legion Patria Nostra The motto of the French Foreign Legion meaning "The Legion is our Homeland."

Leeward On or close to the side sheltered from the wind.

Machine gun A gun that fires bullets very quickly, the bullets often being fed from a long belt.

Mirages Illusion created by heat rising from the desert floor, which distort the air and create the appearance of objects that actually do not exist.

Mortars Weapons that fire bombs in a high arc over long distances, often used by the Legion.

Purification tablets Tablets or powders dropped into water to make the water safe to drink.

Rabies A disease that is passed to humans through the bite of a diseased animal. It will kill the victim unless he or she is treated very quickly.

Solar still A method of collecting water in which drops of condensation are collected each morning in a plastic sheet.

Southern Cross A group of stars in the night sky that are always in the south, and which can be used for navigation.

Square miles The number of miles obtained when you multiply the length by the width.

Vichy The French government, which was on the side of the Germans during the German occupation of France during World War II.

Viet Minh The guerrillas who fought against the French in Indochina between 1945 and 1954.

EQUIPMENT REQUIREMENTS

Headwear
Hat with wide brim
Arab headdress
Scarf/neckcloth (to soak up sweat, and control temperature)

Clothing
Long-sleeved shirts (preferably white to reflect the sun)
Shorts
Jacket/fleece (for night-time wear)
Many pairs of socks
Dark sunglasses/sun goggles

Footwear
Walking boots
Sandals
Spare shoelaces

Load-carrying equipment
Backpack
Small carry sack

Survival Equipment
Medical pack
Sunblock
Mess pack and knife/fork/spoon
Water bottle and mug
Survival knife
Lockable/retractable knife
Tent
Sleeping bag
Plastic sheeting (to build shelters and make solar stills)
Sleeping mat
Telescopic walking stick
Shovel/spade (foldable)
Compass
Watch
Chronograph
Flares
Signaling mirror (heliograph)
Binoculars
Map case
Wash pack
Matches
Flint and steel firelighter
Snare wire
Whistle
Wire saw
Candle
Needles
Water purification tablets

CHRONOLOGY

March 10, 1831	The French Foreign Legion is created by royal ordinance.
1855–1863	The Legion fights in the Crimea (1855), Italy (1859), and Mexico (1863).
April 29, 1863	65 Legionnaires fight against 2,000 Mexican soldiers in the deserted hamlet of Camerone.
1870–1914	Many foreigners join the Legion. It goes on to fight in France itself, Tonkin, Sudan, Dahomey, Madagascar, and Morocco.
1914–1918	World War I. Many legionnaires are killed. All the regiments are brought together into one: the Foreign Legion's "Regiment de Marche." This is commanded by Colonel Rollet, the "Father of the Legion."
1939–1945	World War II. The Legion fights throughout the war in many different places, including Norway, Libya, Tunisia, Germany, and Indochina.
1945–1954	The Indochina War. All regiments of the Legion fight in Indochina.
1969–1970	Two Legion regiments take part in operations in Chad, Africa.
April 3, 1976	Legion paratroopers help the rescue of French schoolchildren held on a bus on the Somali border.
May 1978	2nd Foreign Parachute Regiment rescues thousands of European and African hostages at Kolwezi, Zaire.
1990–1991	Legion soldiers fight during the Gulf War as part of the Allied force against Iraq.
1994	Peacekeeping operations in Rwanda.
1995	Foreign Legion units are deployed to Bosnia, Yugoslavia, on peacekeeping operations.
1995–2001	The Foreign Legion maintains a strong presence throughout Africa, conducting many peacekeeping and humanitarian operations.

RECRUITMENT INFORMATION

To join the Foreign Legion you need to be between 17 and 40 years old; physically fit; and have an official passport. You do not need to know the French language when you join—but all Legionnaires are taught French.

How to join:
Go to any Legion recruitment office in France. If you are accepted for training, you will be sent to the Legion Headquarters in Aubagne, France. Once there, you will spend three weeks undergoing medical exams, security checks, aptitude tests, and interviews. You are not permitted contact with the outside world while in Aubagne and cannot phone or write anyone. If you pass this stage, you then have to sign a five-year contract with the Legion. You will then receive four months of basic training before being sent on to your new regiment.

Acceptance
Indicators of being a successful candidate are: a colored tab they give you to wear that progresses from yellow to green and finally to red; a haircut—haircuts are not given until several phases of indoctrination are complete; being assigned a six-digit serial number that you need to memorize and recite; a final interview where you are asked why you want to join the French Foreign Legion; and being outfitted with the military gear you will need for basic training and your regiment.

Useful web sites:
http://www.frenchforeignlegion.org
http://frenchforeignlegionlife.com
http://www.angelfire.com/fl/marcwitteveen
http://www.consulfrance-newyork.org/alegion.htm
http://www.info-france-usa.org/america/embassy/legion/legion.htm
http://www.foreignlegionlife.com/
http://www.geocities.com/~jmgould/legion.html
http://www.azuswebworks.com/oldhtml/desertsurvival.html

FURTHER READING

Alloway, David. *Desert Survival Skills*. Dallas, Tex.: University of Texas Press, 2000.

Fessler, Diane M. (editor). *Desert Survival Handbook: How to Prevent and Handle Emergency Situations*. London: Primer, 1998.

Grubbs, Bruce. *Desert Hiking Tips*. Helena, Mon.: Falcon Publishing Company, 1999.

McGorman, Evan. *Life in the French Foreign Legion: How to Join and What to Expect When You Get There*. Central Point, Ore.: Hellgate Press, 2000.

Parker, John. *Inside the Foreign Legion: The Sensational Story of the World's Toughest Army*. London: London Bridge Trade, 2000.

Porch, Douglas. *The French Foreign Legion: A Complete History of the Legendary Fighting Force*. New York: HarperPerennial Library, 1992.

Simpson, Howard R. *The Paratroopers of the French Foreign Legion: From Vietnam to Bosnia*. Dulles, Va.: Brasseys Inc., 1999.

Stillwell, Alexander. *The Encyclopedia of Survival Techniques*. New York: Lyons Press, 2000.

ABOUT THE AUTHOR

Dr. Chris McNab has written and edited numerous books on military history and elite forces survival. His list of publications to date includes *German Paratroopers of World War II*, *The Illustrated History of the Vietnam War*, *First Aid Survival Manual*, and *Special Forces Endurance Techniques*. His wider research interests lie in literature and ancient history. Chris lives in South Wales, U.K.

INDEX

References in italics refer to illustrations